COFFEE
TALK

T
TEAM BUILDING
SCHOOL
FEATURING TYLER HAYDEN

Coffee Talk, A Nano Sized Team Building Game

Published by Tyler Hayden,
Lunenburg, Nova Scotia
Canada

Cover: Tyler Hayden
Illustrations & Page Design: Steven Lacey
Distributed by Kindle Direct Publishing

Notional Library of Canada Cataloguing in Publication Hayden, Tyler, 1974-
Coffee Talk: A Nano Sized Team Building Game / Tyler Hayden.

E-Book ISBN 978-1-897050-81-1
Print ISBN 978-1-897050-80-4

Business. 2. Education. 3. Games. I. Title.

Coffee Talk
By Tyler Hayden

Warning - Use at Your Own Risk

Improper use of the contents described herein may result in serious injury or loss. The activities should not be attempted without the supervision of a trained and properly qualified leader.

Neither the author, publisher, seller or any distributor of this publication assumes any liability for loss or damage, direct or consequential to the reader or others resulting from the use of the materials contained herein, whether such loss or damages results from errors, omissions, ambiguities or inaccuracies in the materials contained herein or otherwise. No warranties, express or implied, as to the merchantability or as to fitness for any particular use or purpose are intended to arise out of the sole or distribution of this publication and this publication is sold "as is" and "with ail faults." The liability of the author, publisher, seller, or any distributor of this publication on account of any such errors, omissions, or ambiguities, scale in any event, be limited to the purchase price of this publication.

All rights reserved. No part of this publication may be reproduced, stored in a retrieval system or transmitted in any form or by any means, electronic, mechanical, photocopying, recording, or otherwise, without the prior written permission of the owner.

FIND THIS FOR FREE ... WANT TO GIVE US A HIGH FIVE TO SAY THANK YOU?

We'd love you to BUY US A COFFEE or four - we like coffee. Head over to **www.teambuildingschool.com** and purchase your copy today.

How to Play ...

Coffee Talk, By Tyler Hayden

This game takes about 10 to 25 minutes to play. It is an incredible icebreaker/ break-time activity that is totally inclusive. The educational intention is to encourage people to know a little more about each other in a fun and interactive way. It is also a great deinhibitizer for team dialogue and communication.

Remember, the priorities are to have fun and play safe.

How to play:

1. Invite your team to gather (at a staff meeting, retreat, or informally in the lunchroom) and ask them if they would like to take a 15-minute break.

2. Pull out a copy of Coffee Talk and explain how to play the game. Start by having everyone grab a coffee (or beverage of their choice) and sit around a table or in a circle.

3. The person who has the longest hair goes first. They will flip the card page to reveal a question, then read the question aloud to the group.

4. Everyone in the group will take turns answering questions, once the person is finished answering their question, they pass the device to the person on their left. Repeat until everyone has had a chance to answer the question.

5. Play as long as time permits or stop when people are having the most amount of fun

Discover More Fun @ www.teambuildingschool.com

The best attribute I bring to this team is ...

My Mom taught me

...

Where do you go to relax? Why is that the place you choose?

The best skill I bring to the team is ...

I am most motivated when ...

What is one thing that your parents were right about, but you hate to admit they were?

What are your thoughts on UFO's and extraterrestrial life forms?

What is your greatest success so far in life?

If I could have dinner with one famous person (alive or dead) it would be ...

What is your all time favourite movie? Why?

What is the most important thing in your life right now? Why?

My greatest hero or heroine is ... because ...

The think I'm looking forward to the most about working with this team is ...

What is one thing people wouldn't know about you, that would be surprising that you would like to share?

Who is your favourite musician?

If you could stop a world crisis what one would it be? Why?

Who is your greatest role model?

The best thing that happened to me this week is ..

My family is ...

If I could do another job other than the one I'm currently in I would love to ...

What is your fondest memory of your children or of when you were a child?

My Dad taught me

...

How do you think they got the caramel inside the Caramilk Bar?

If you could have one "do-over" in life, what would it be?

What do you see yourself doing two years from now?

My dream vacation is ...

If you could bronze a part of your body, what would you choose and why?

What is the most "off the wall, spur of the moment" thing you have ever done?

My greatest strength is ...

My favourite part of my job is ...

My favourite possession is ...

I eat Chunky soup with a ... (fork or spoon)

What holiday do you go all out for? (Halloween, Valentines, etc.)

The one thing I hate to do at work is ...

If you won $10 million, what would you do with it?

What is your greatest passion?

What is the most life defining moment for you so far?

My kids taught me

...

What is your favourite saying or quote?

What is your favourite TV show? Why?

If you could be on one reality TV show, which one and why?

What are your 3 major goals right now?

What is your favourite game to play?

What is one thing that just gets on your nerves?

What has been your biggest challenge in life that you have been able to overcome?

Who is the most famous person you have ever met?

What is the coolest place you have ever visited?

If you could blow $1000 on anything, what would you spend it on?

The greatest reward or recognition that I like to receive for a job well done is ...

Currently I volunteer my time for the ...

What qualities do you respect and admire in people the most?

The weirdest thing I've ever purchased is ...

In my "free time" I like to ...

What is your favorite way to spend your time after work or on weekends?

What make of car best describes your personality?

If I could have dinner with one famous person (alive or dead) it would be ...

What song do you like to sing at the top of your lungs?

What app keeps you engaged longest?

Have you ever had any pets? Name them?

What school sports or activities were you involved in?

If someone played you in an autobiography film, who would it be?

If you could be a comic book superhero/ heroine, who would you be?

What is your favourite chore to do around the house?

If you were super rich, what's one thing you'd never do again?

Who was your best friend growing up?

What is one of your life goals?

Where was your first job?

What is your favourite sinful indulgence to eat?

What was the last show you binge watched?

One job I know I never could do is ...

My dream vacation is ...

Right now, I'm feeling ...

I won a prize/ trophy once because I ...

A little-known fact about me is ...

To me cooking is ...

The first time I drank coffee I ...

When people come to my house, we hang out in the ... because ...

The one thing that I always procrastinate doing is ...

The fanciest meal I have ever made was ...

My famous person crush was ... (or is) ...

If I ruled the country, the one thing I would change is ...

The one machine or tool in my home I couldn't live without is ... because ...

If I were an artist I'd love to create using the medium

...

The recreational activity I like to do is ...

The thing I love most about where I live is ...

If I could take one course, I would learn how to ...

A moment in history I would have liked to be part of was ...

The furthest away place I've ever been was ...

My favourite toy growing up was ...

My favourite type of book to read is ...

If I could own one original piece of art, it would be ...

Thank You for Playing with Us.

Download amazing Team Building
Tools & Take Certificate Courses at:

www.teambuildingschool.com

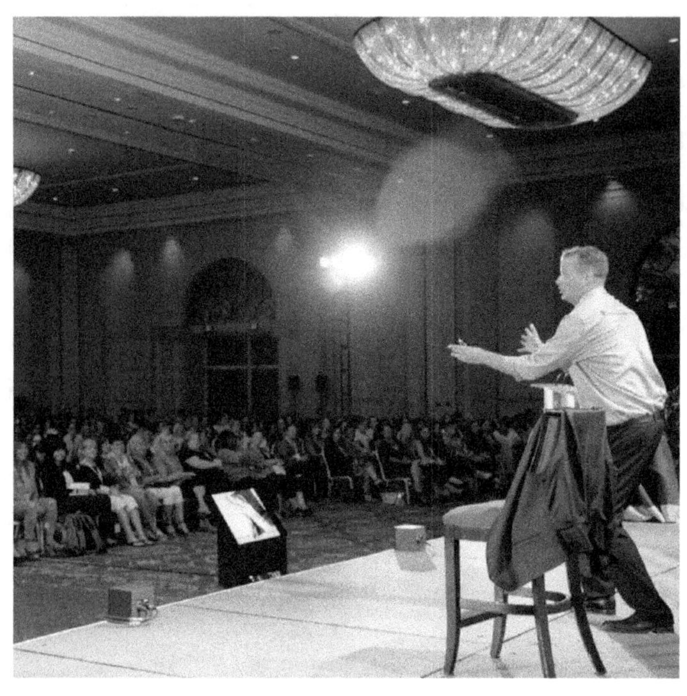

Learn More & book Tyler for your next Keynote or Team Event:

www.tylerhayden.com

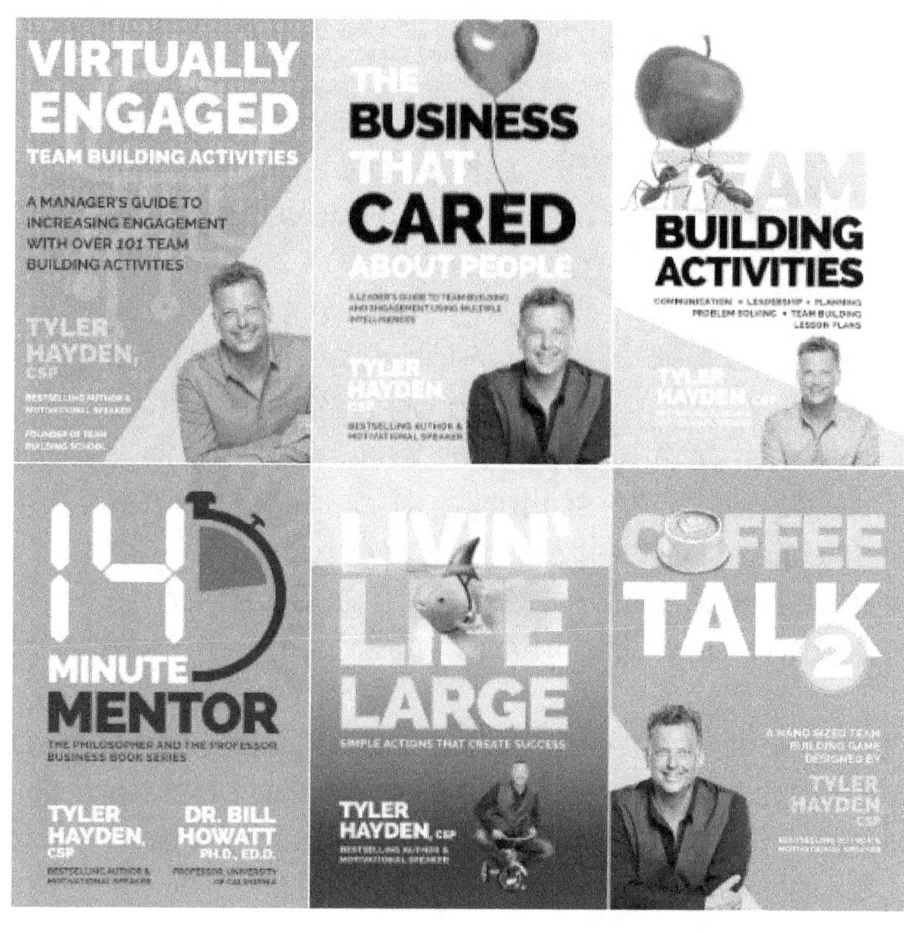

Find more
great books and activities at:

www.tylerhayden.com/shop

Who is this Guy?

Tyler Hayden CSP, is a keynote speaker like you've never experienced before!

Since 1996, Tyler continues to be a sought after internationally respected team building designer, best-selling author, and business speaker. He delivers a powerful punch that inspires teams, innovates management techniques, and invigorates team engagement.

When it comes to empowering audiences and teams to succeed—and to be their best every day—Tyler leads the way with insight and laughter.

His team building workshops and motivational keynote speeches receive rave reviews from managers and business leaders alike. "Energizing," "hilarious," "who knew learning could be this much fun." and "ideas I can easily implement," are things regularly said by Tyler's clients about his keynotes and team building events.

He is the author of over twenty-five books and the creative mind behind 100s of powerful and fun team building products including: Virtually Engaged Team Building Activities, The Business that Cared About People, The 14-Minute Mentor, Livin' Life Large, Father's & Mother's Message in a. Bottle, TEAM Activities, and More.

Tyler is a thought leader who works internationally with Fortune 500, Inc 5000 and Premier Associations to level-up their learning design. Tyler's innovative gamification and in-depth understanding of multiple intelligences yields programs that increase engagement and learning in amazingly simple ways.

Some of his past clients include: Subway, Michelin, Honeywell, YPO, Subaru, TD Bank, Pratt & Whiteny, and more.

Make sure your seat backs are up and your table trays are stowed, because we are about to unleash Canada's Answer to Alternative Energy ...

Invite Tyler to Speak at your Next Event
www.tylerhayden.com

 **Scan to Learn More**

TEAM BUILDING
SCHOOL
FEATURING TYLER HAYDEN